Adult Coloring Book Designs

Calm Your Soul & Mind With These Creative Coloring Book Featuring Mandala and Peaceful Patterns

By Dorothy Mohl

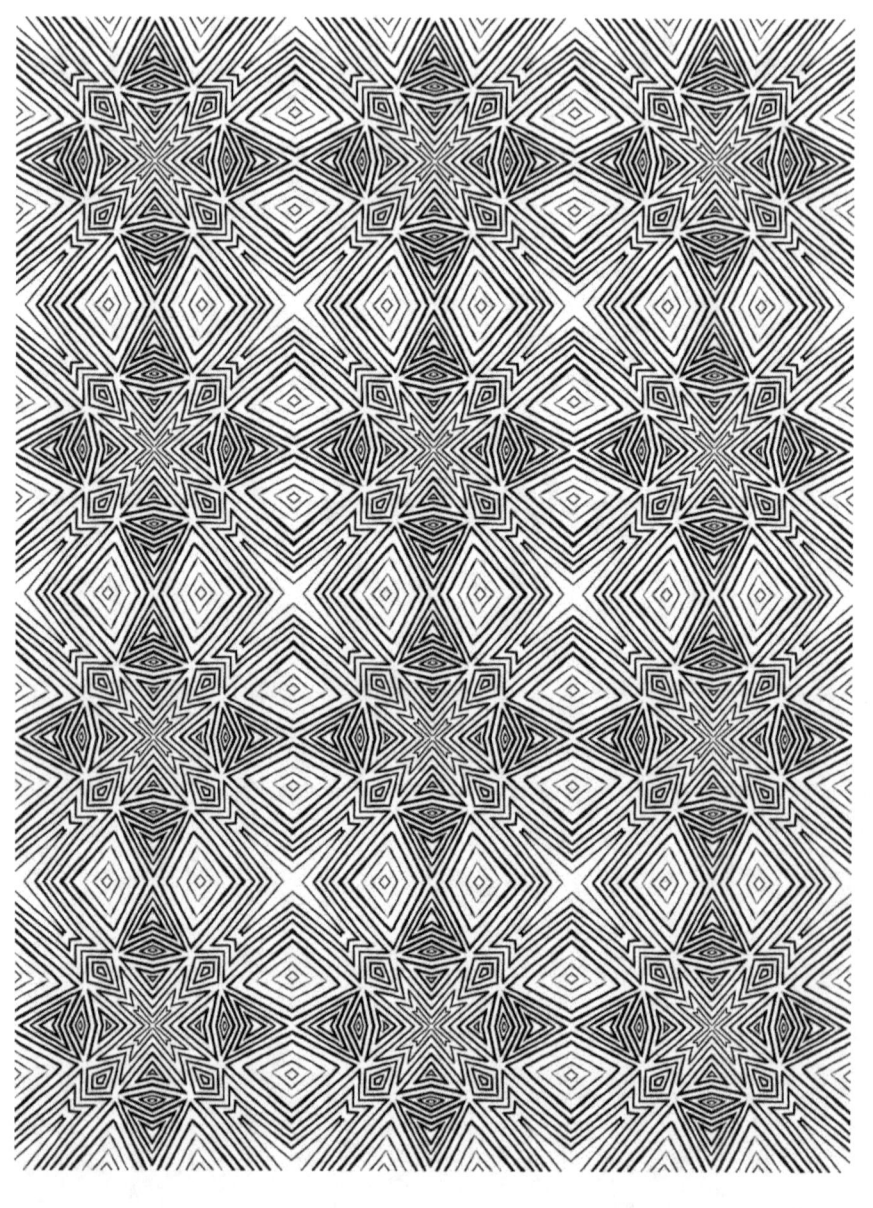

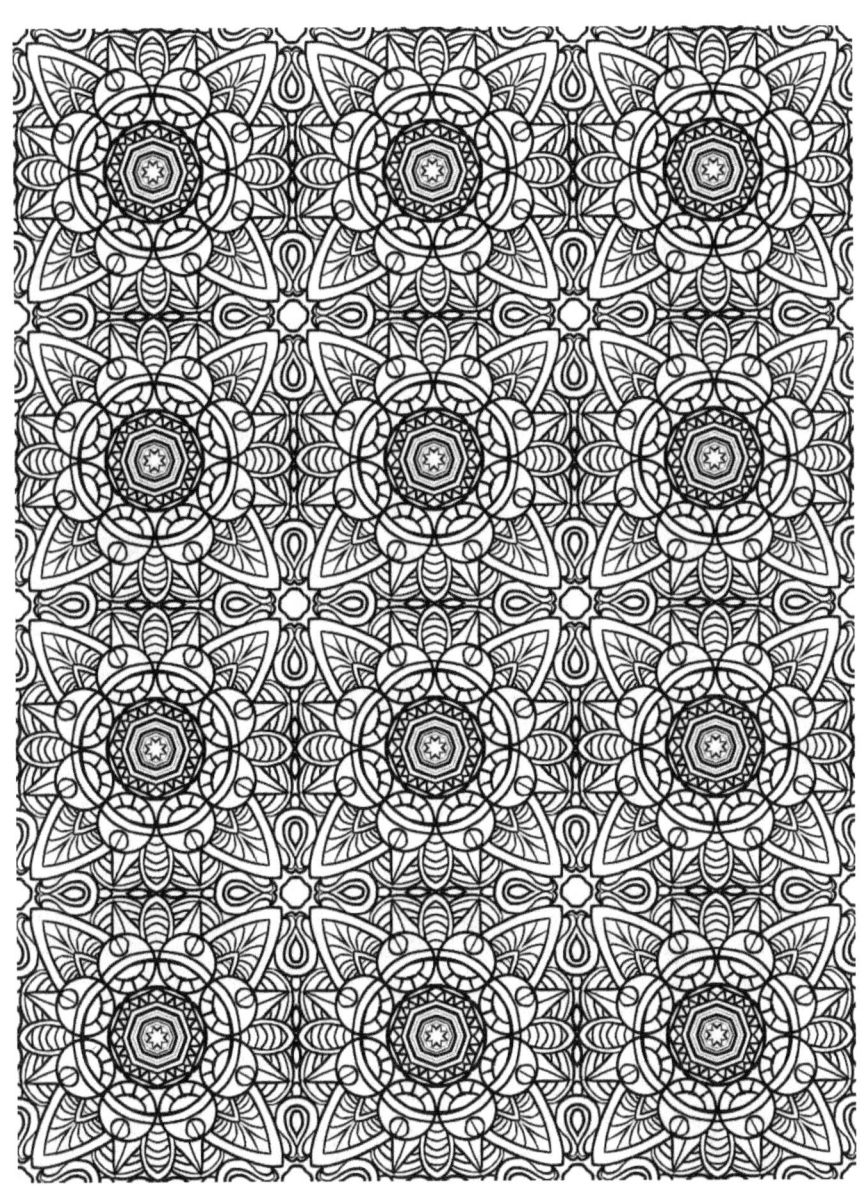

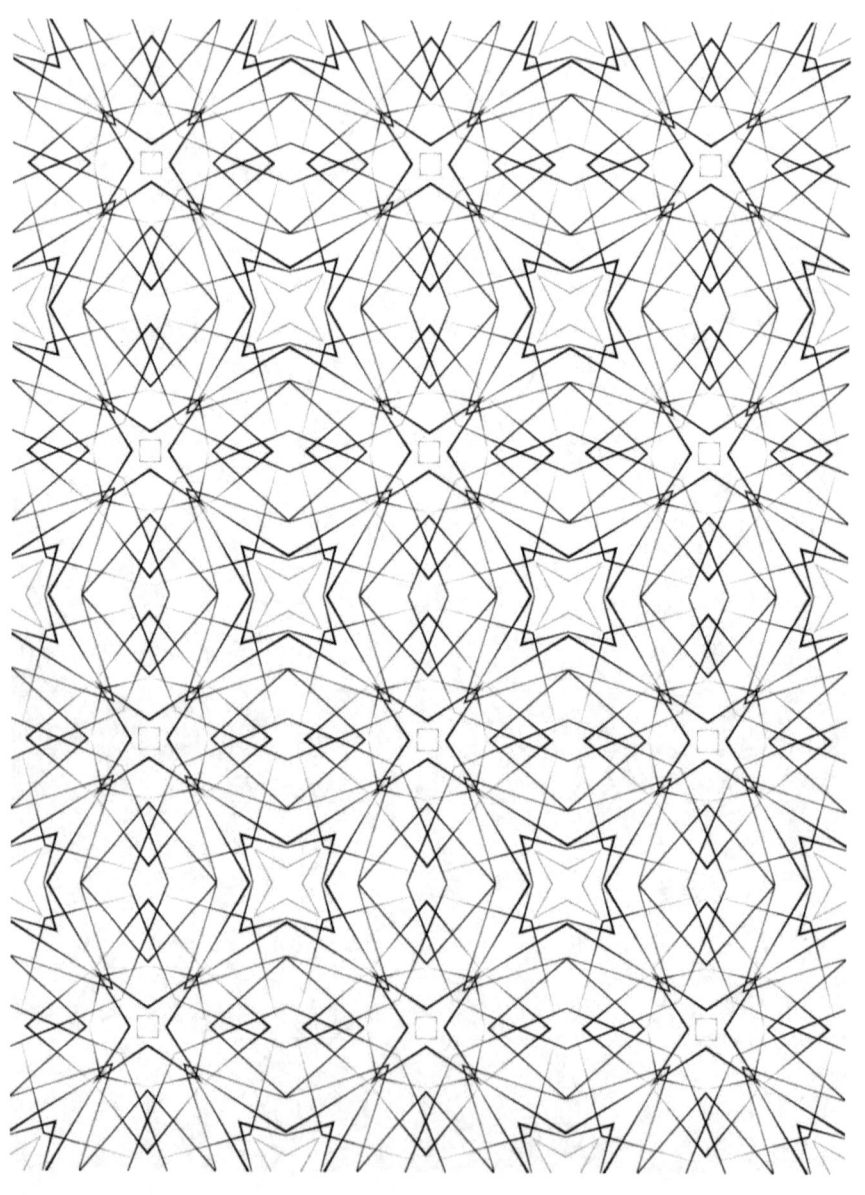

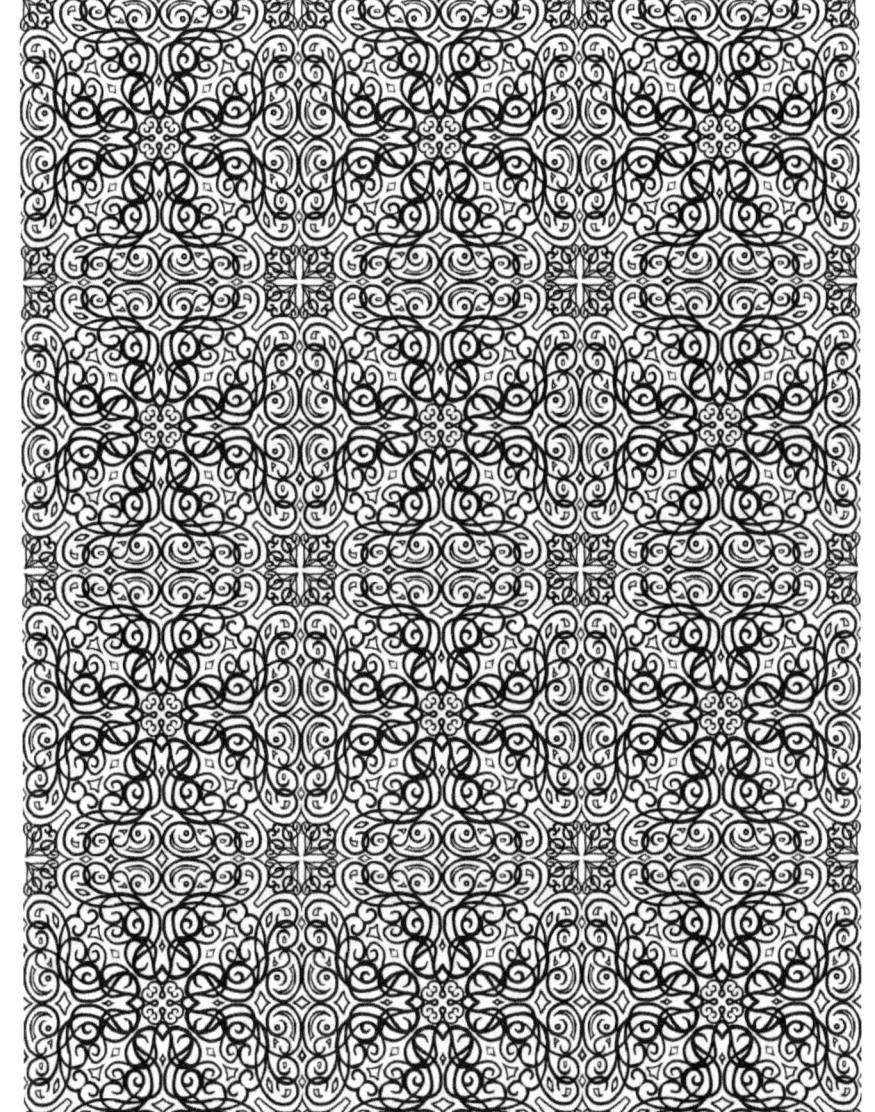

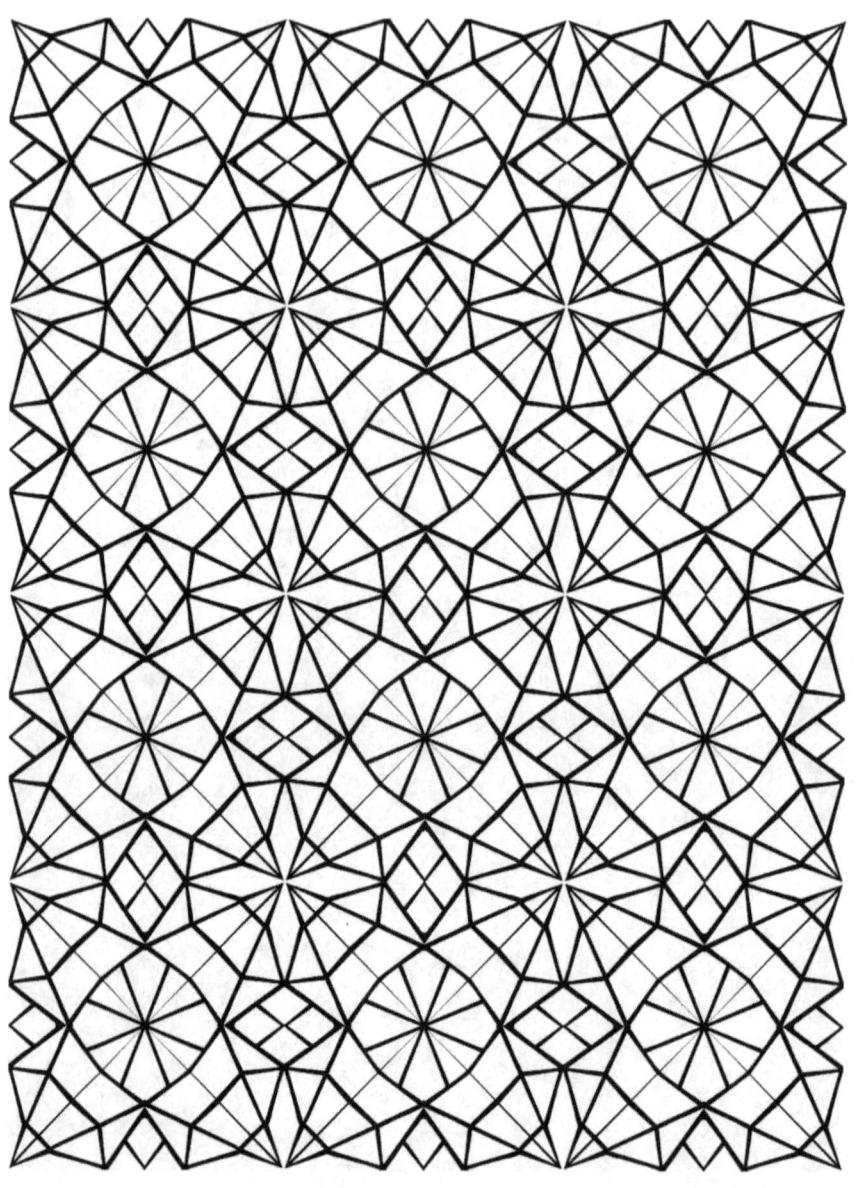

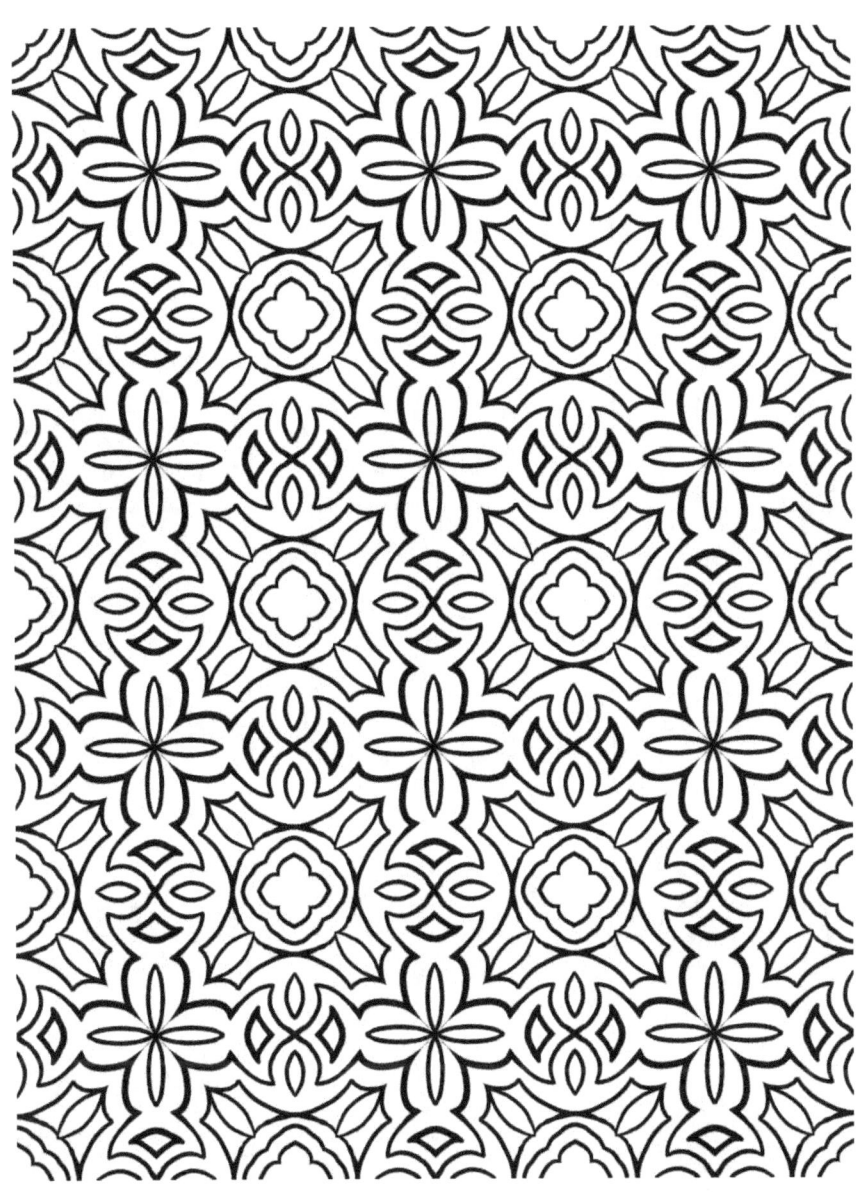

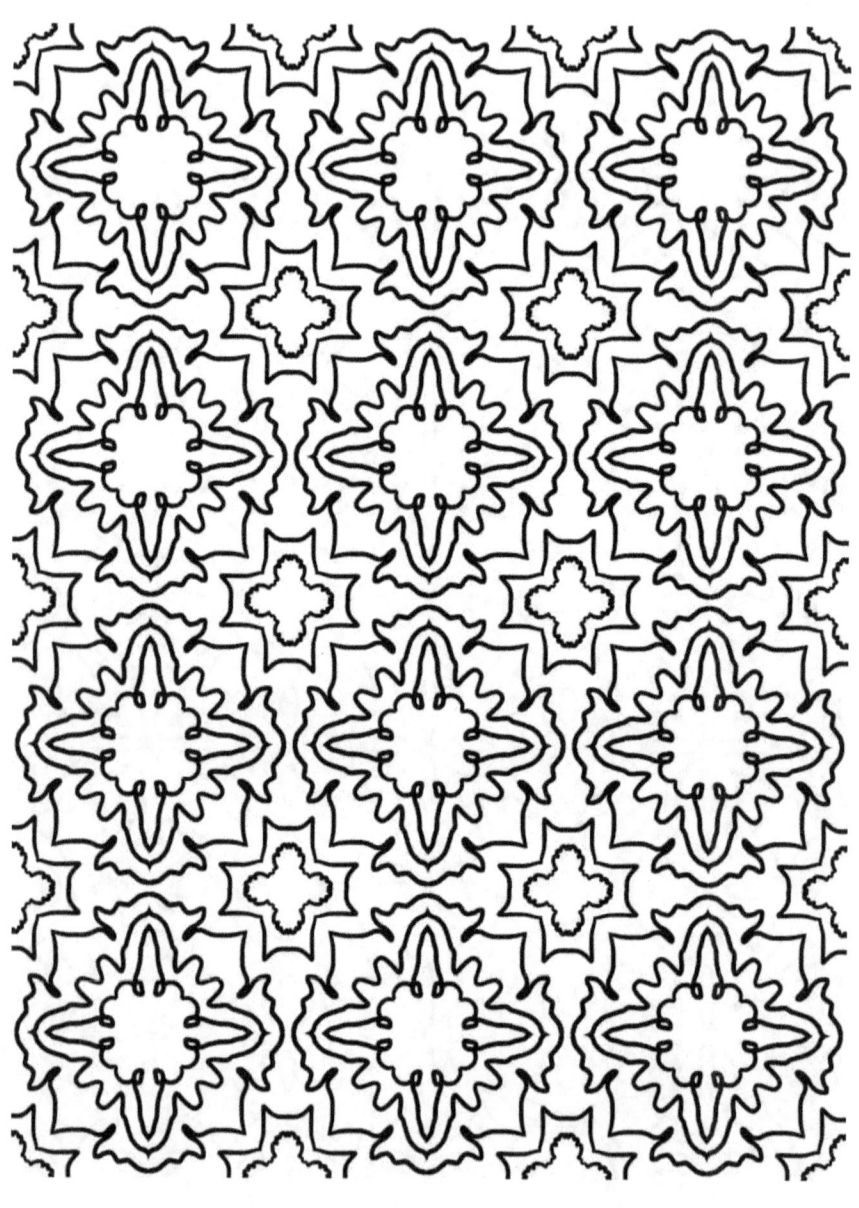

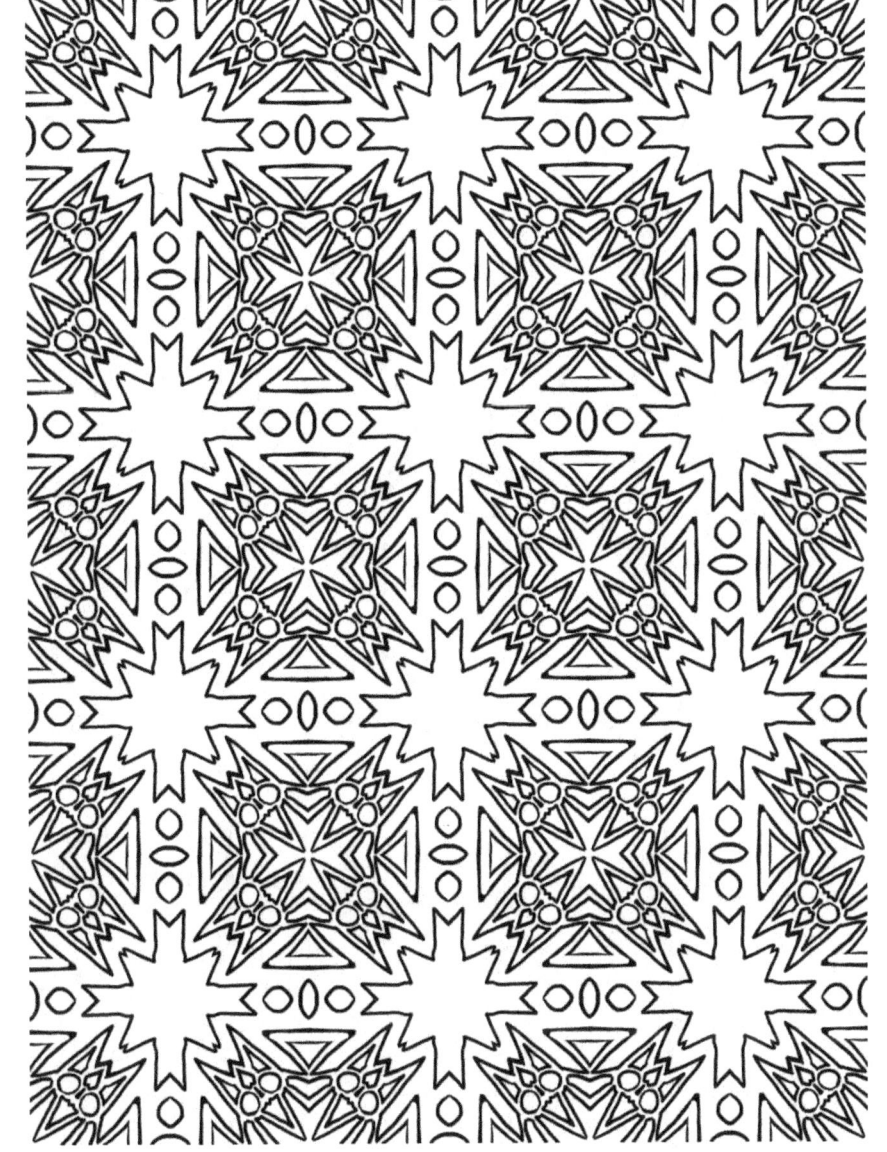

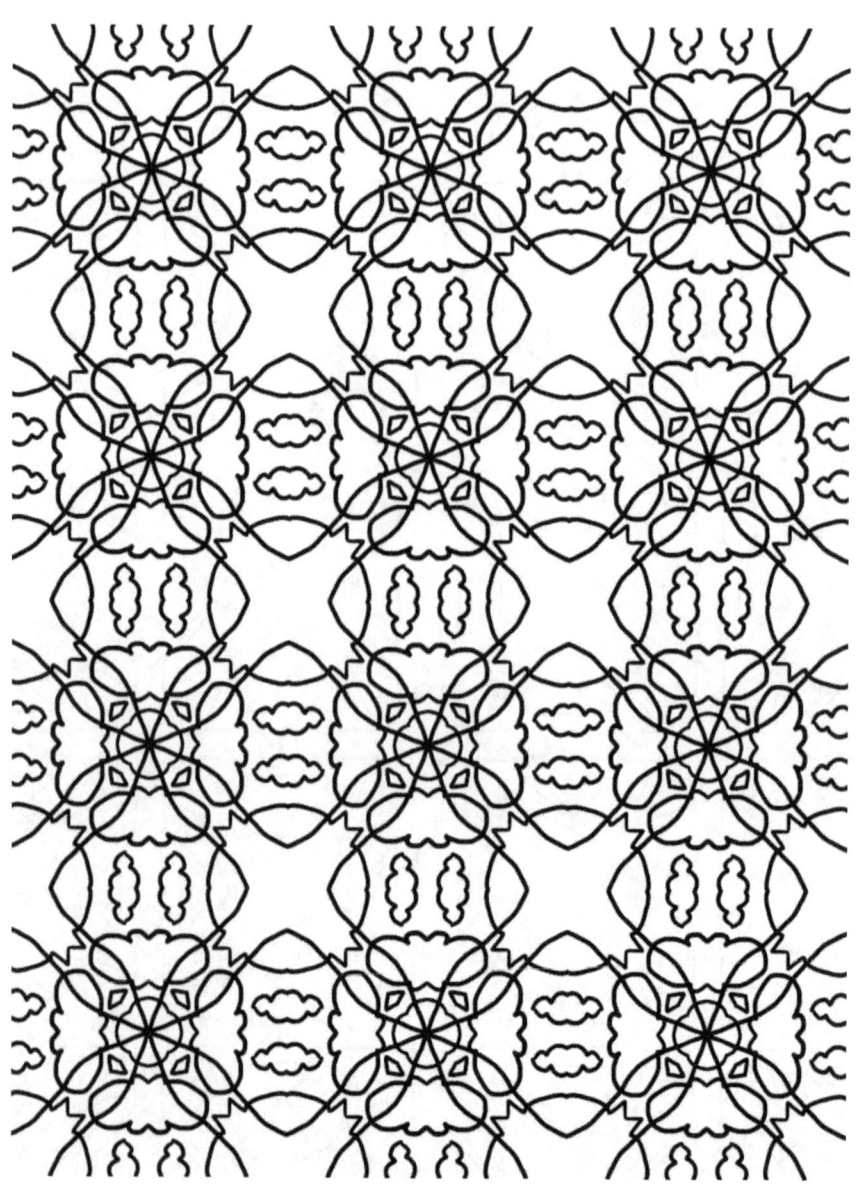

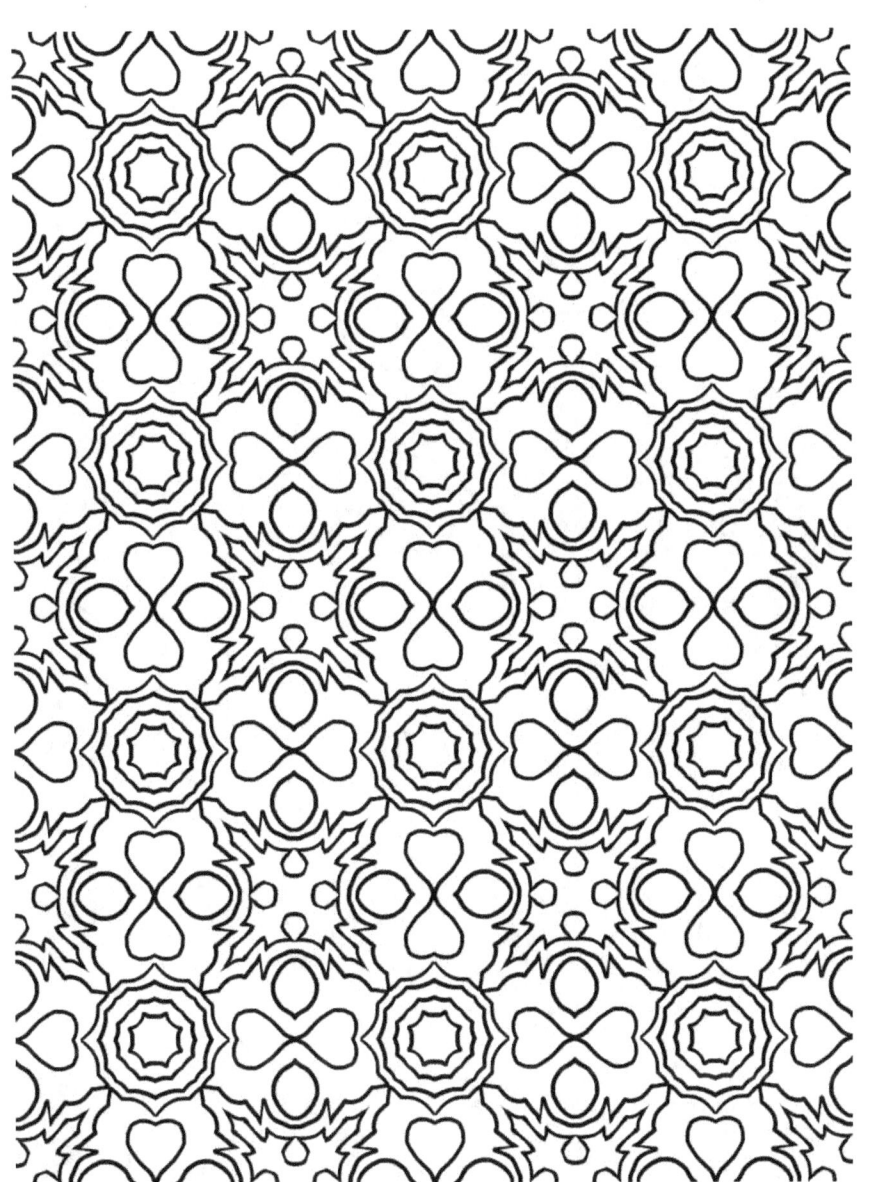

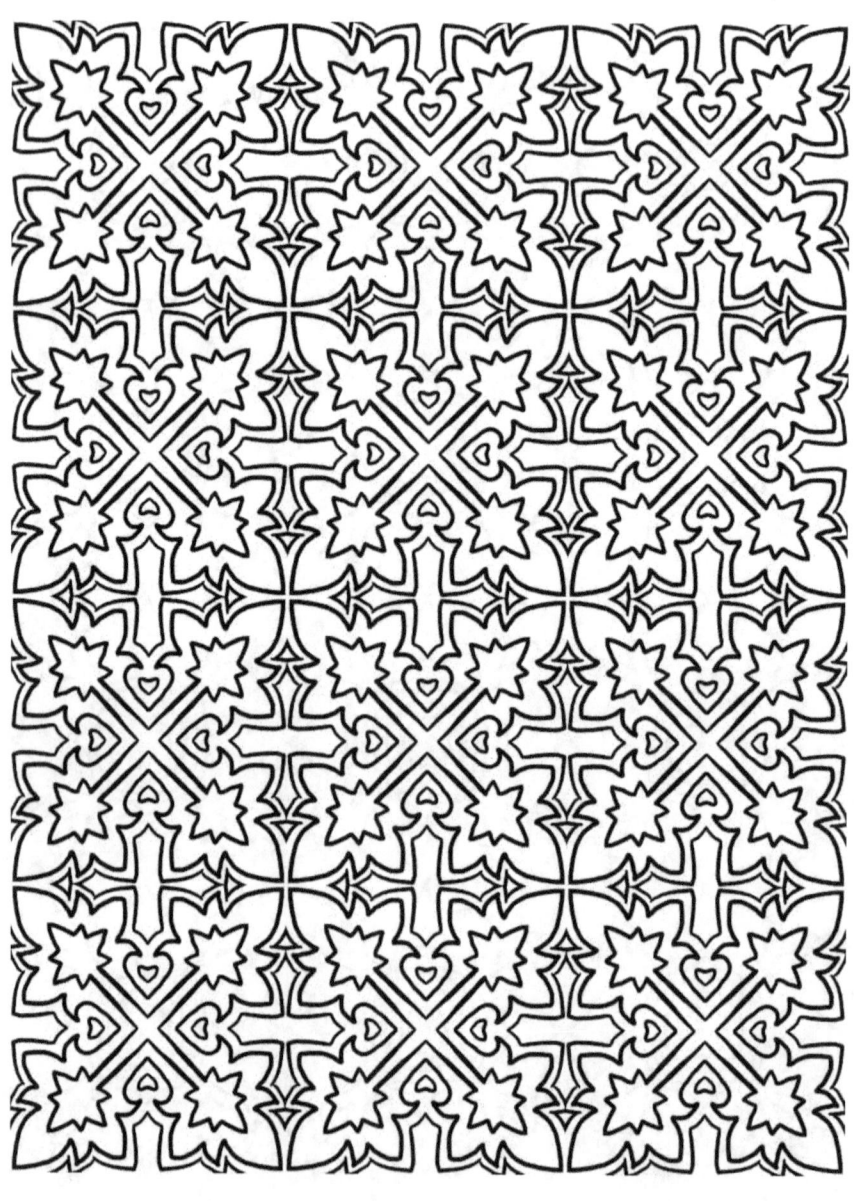

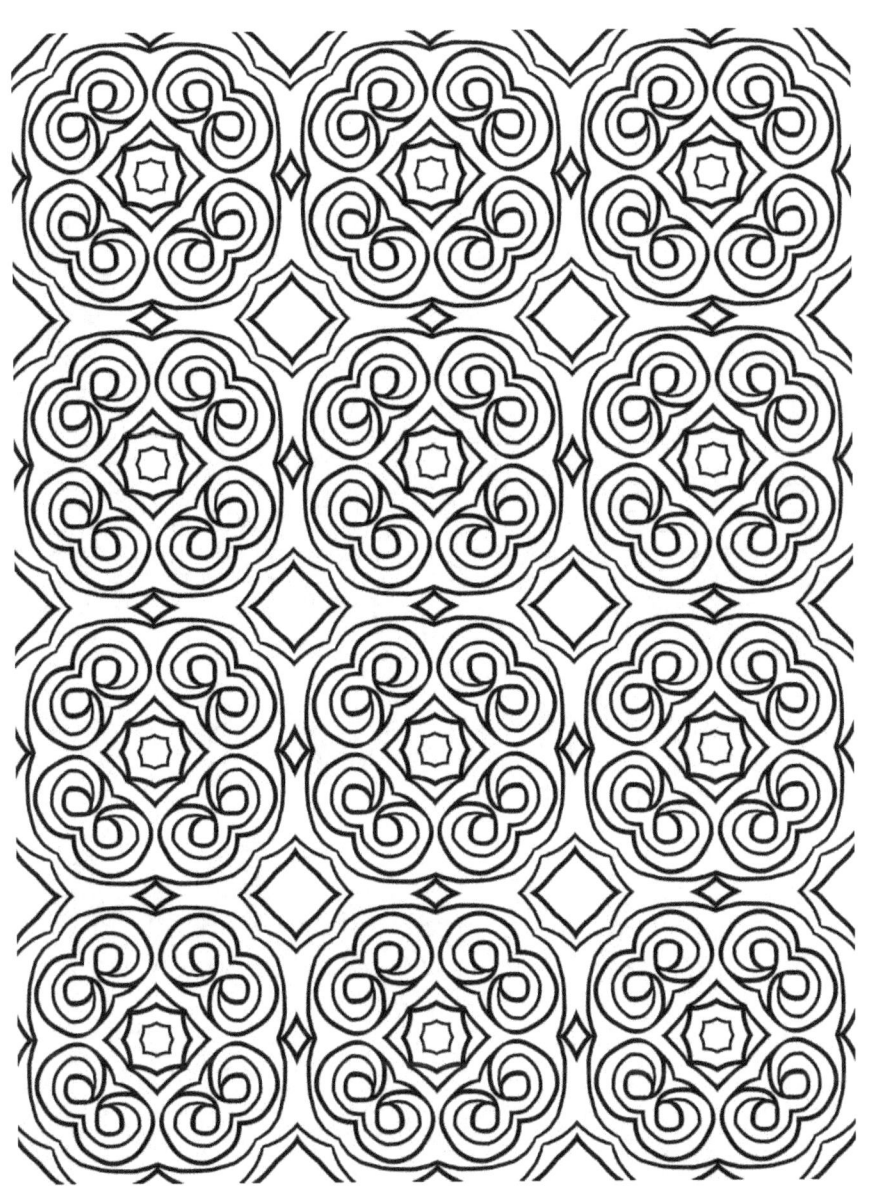

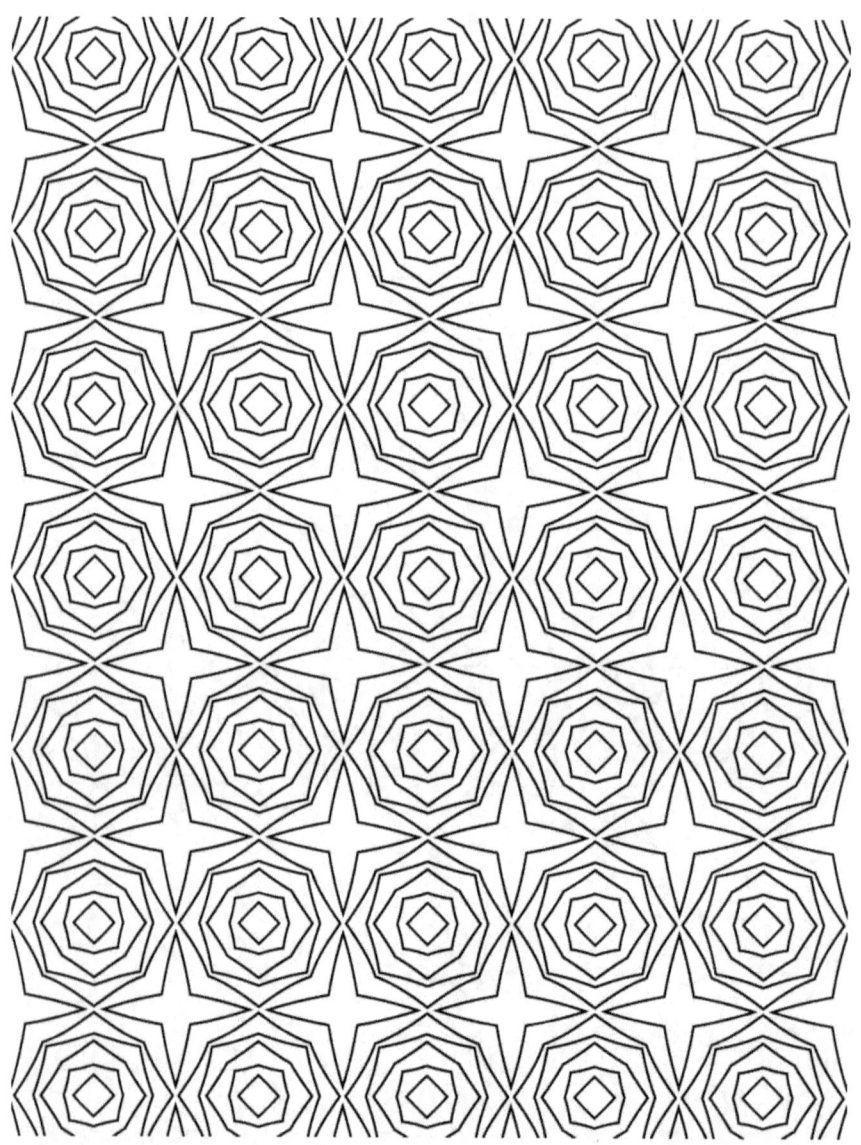

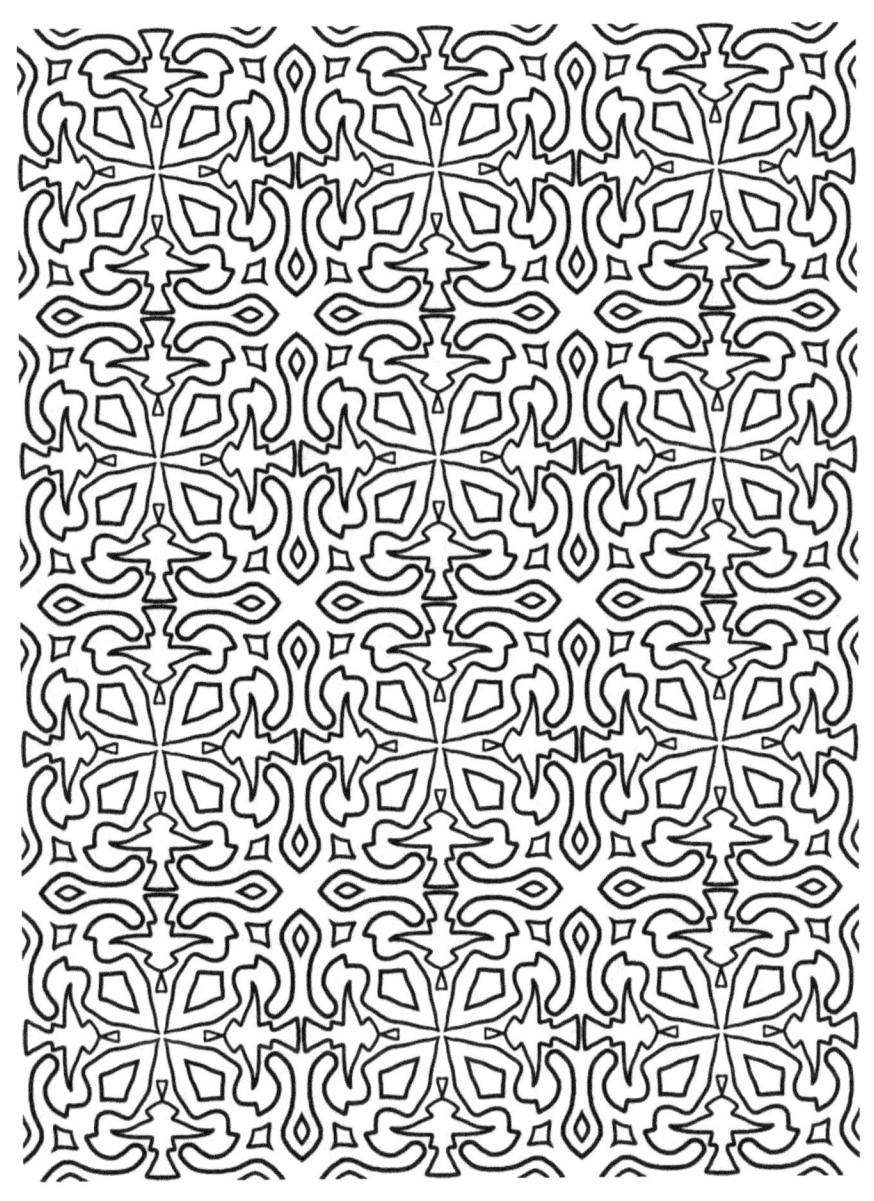

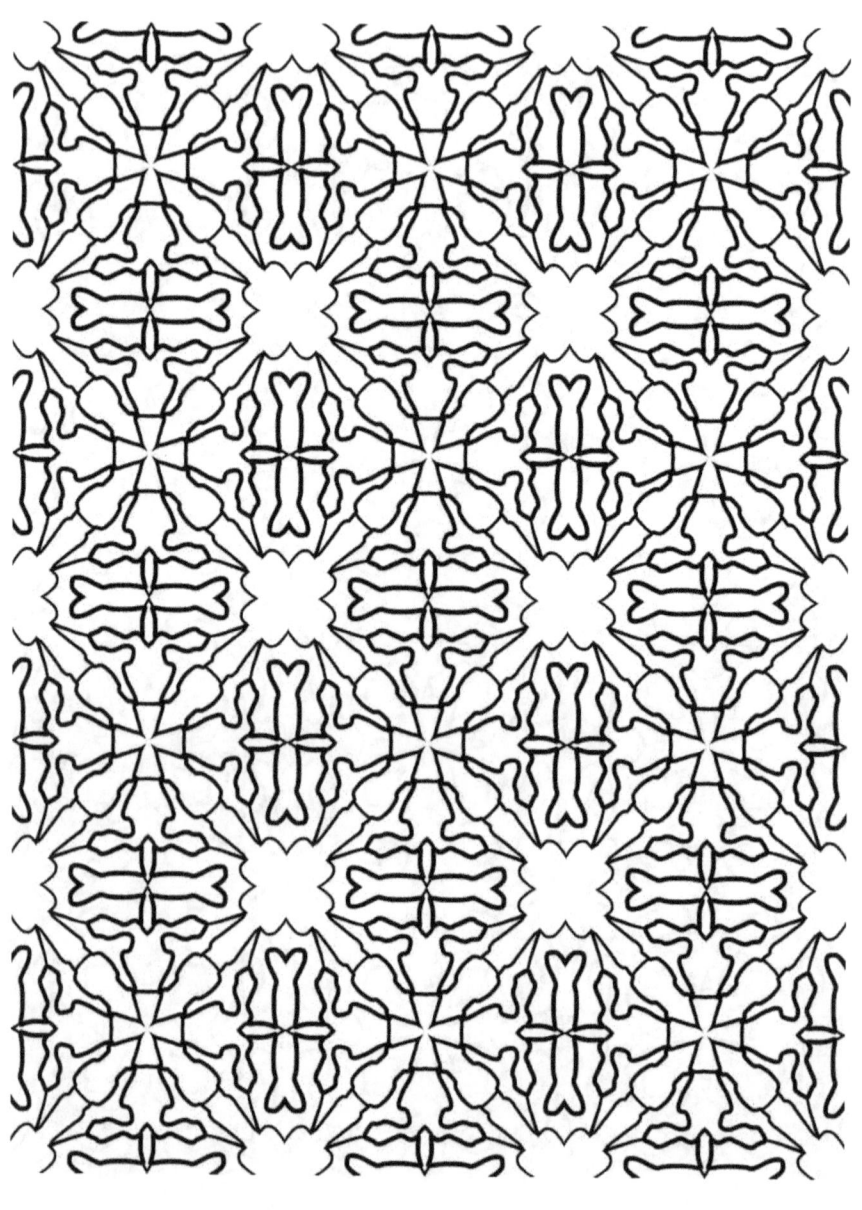

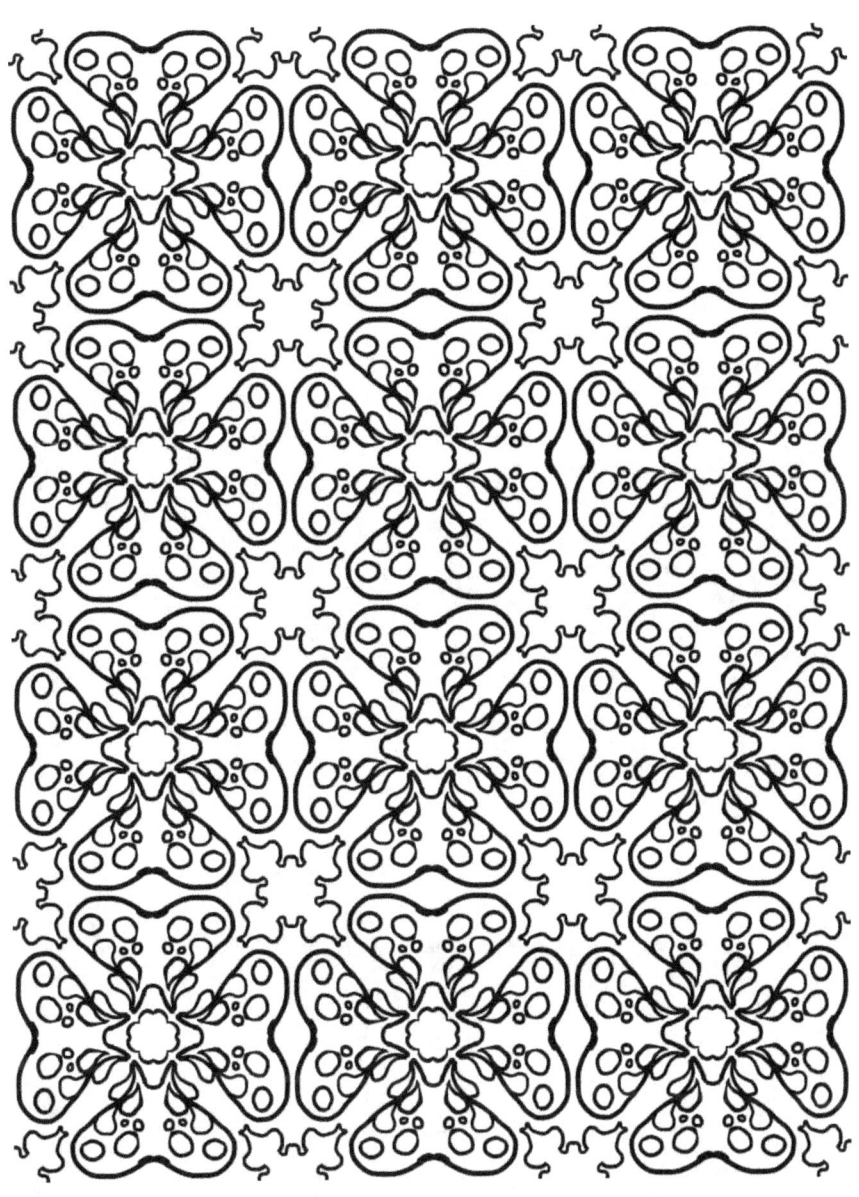

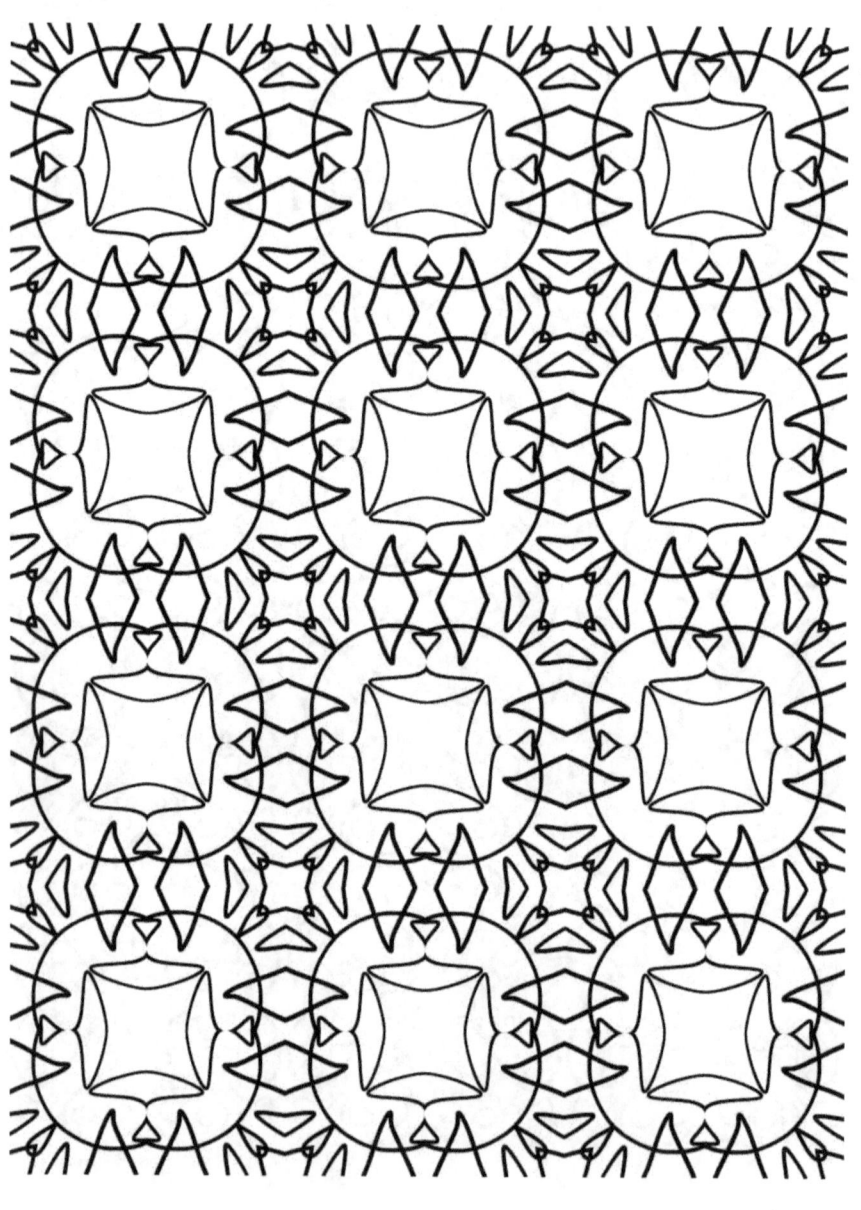

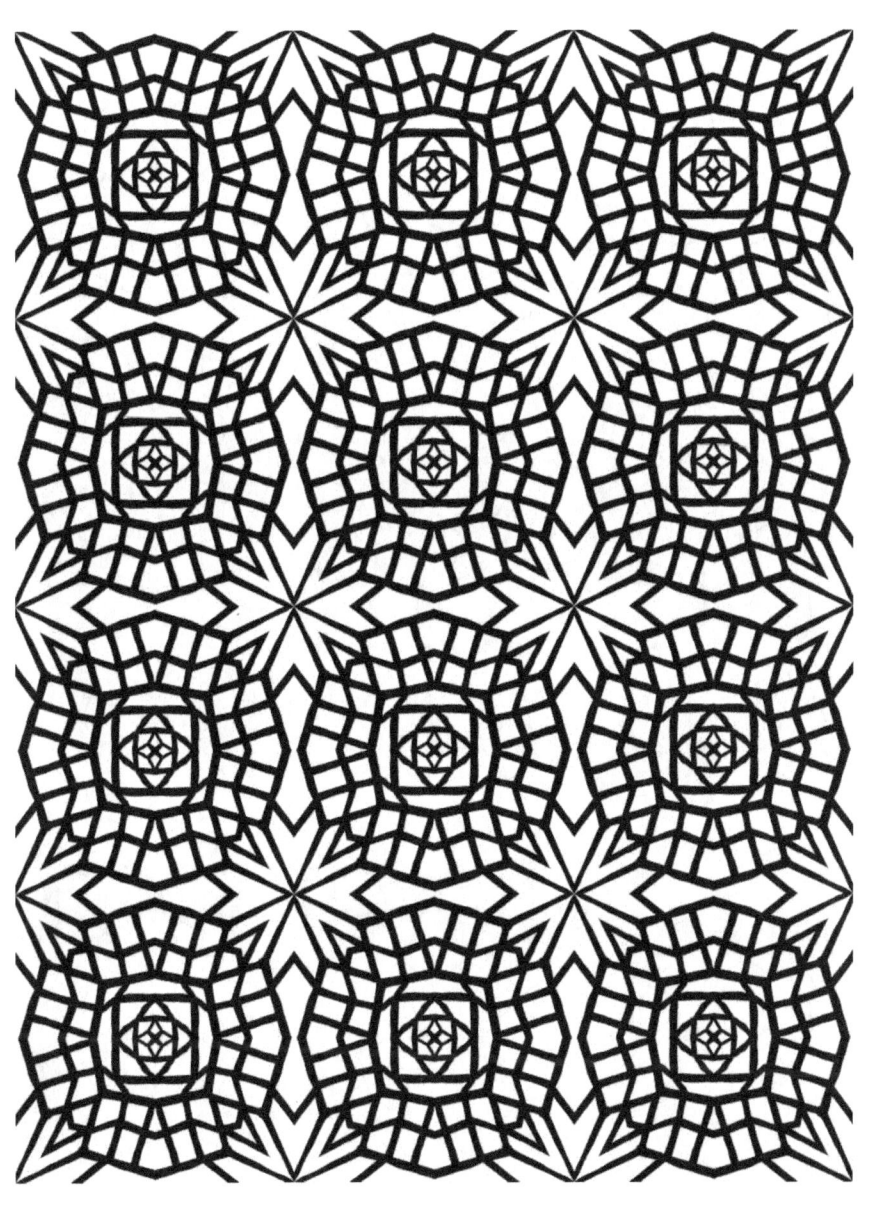

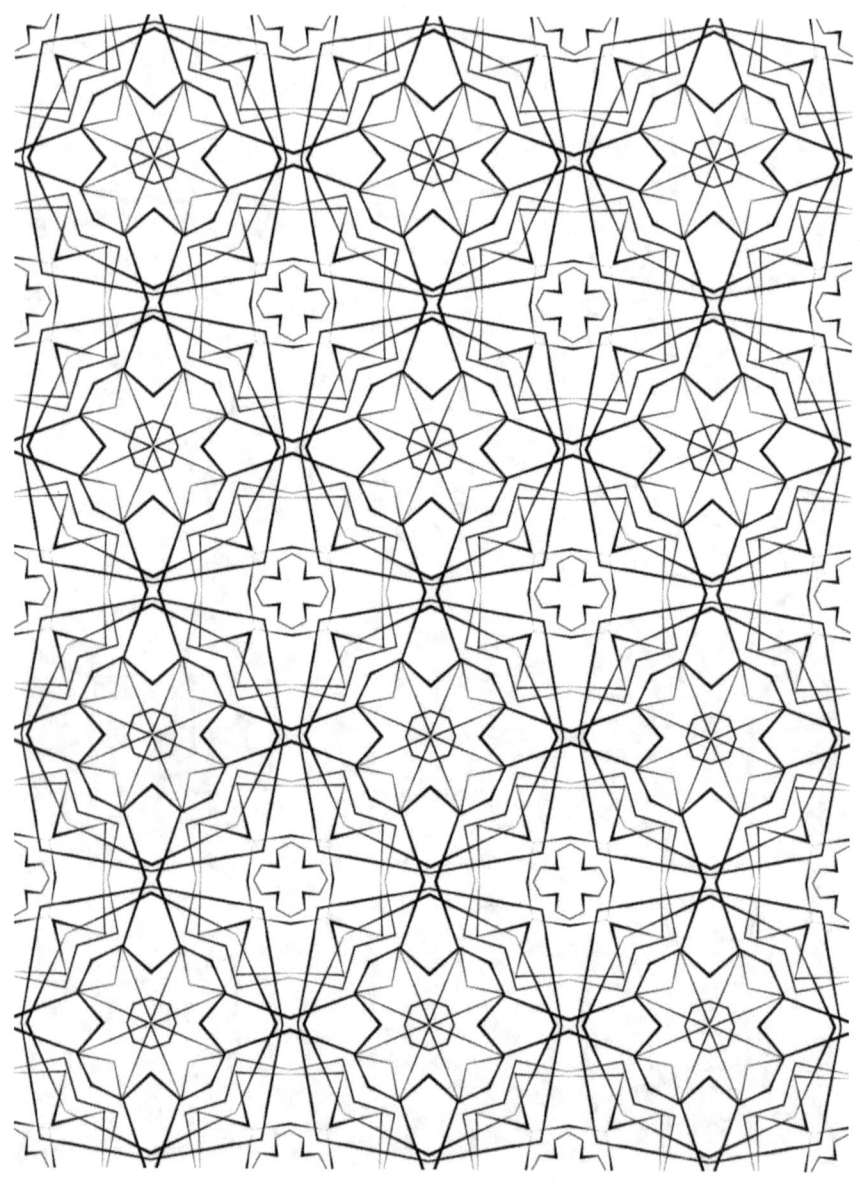

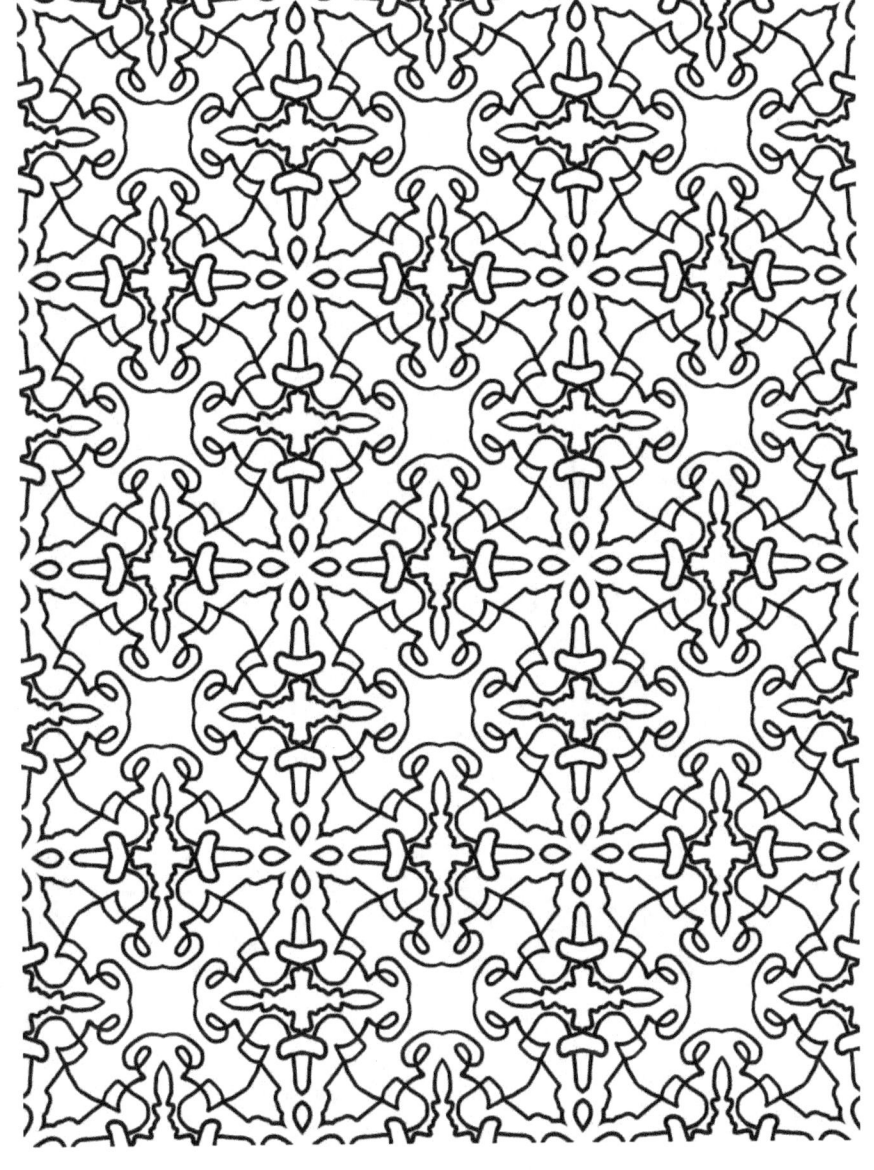

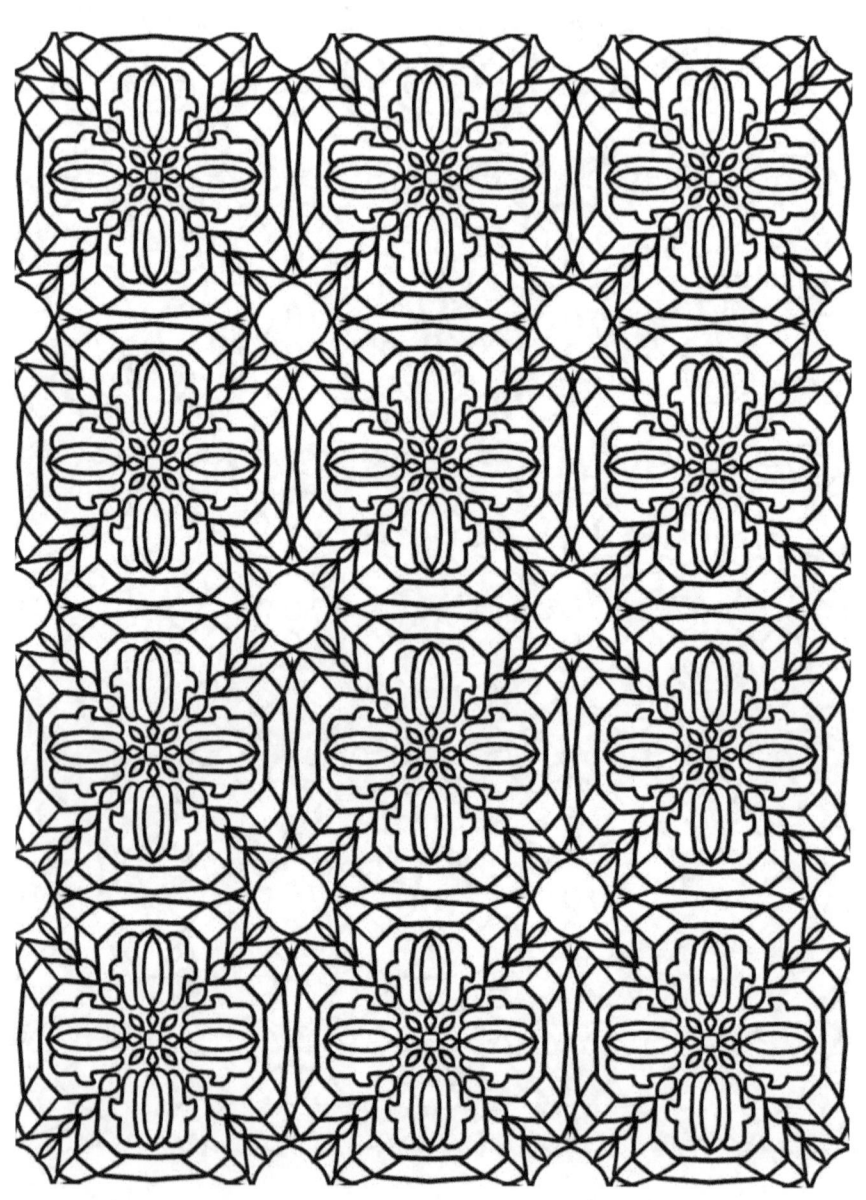

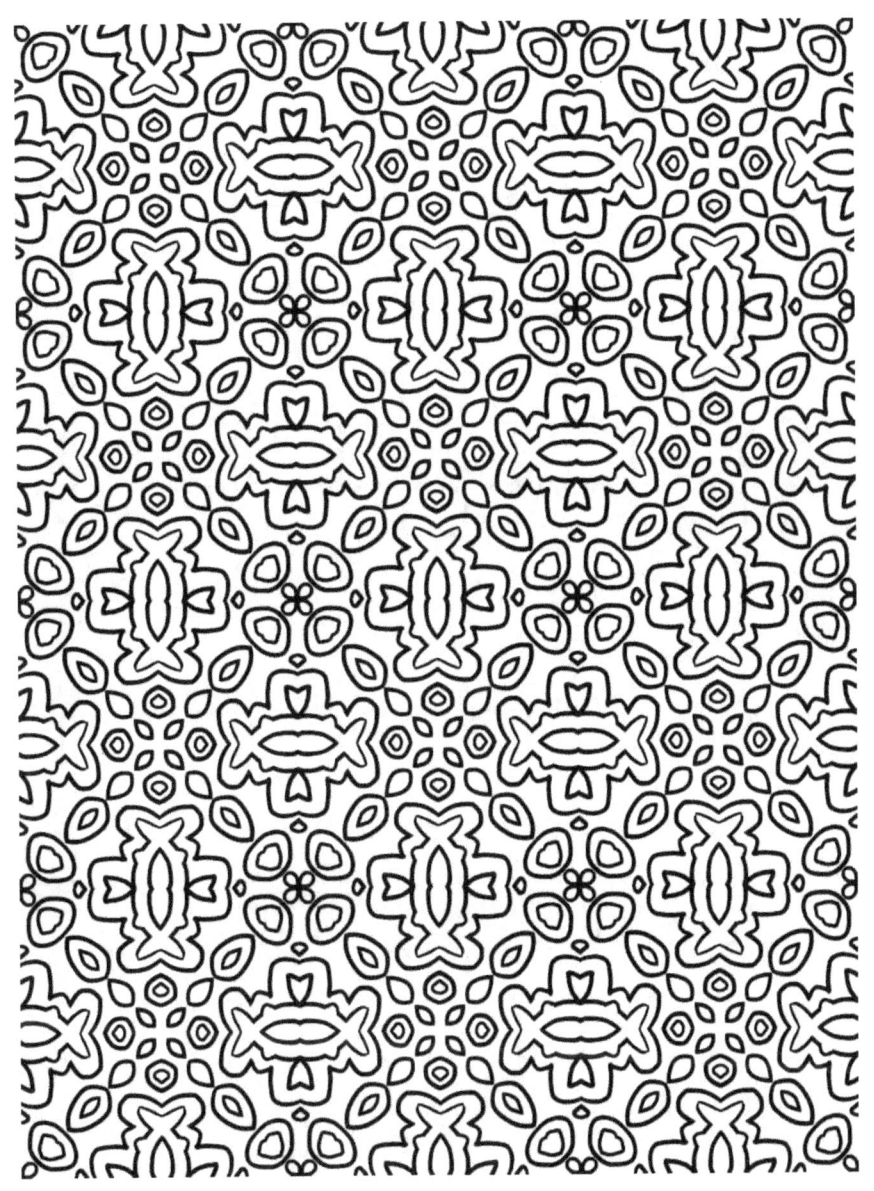

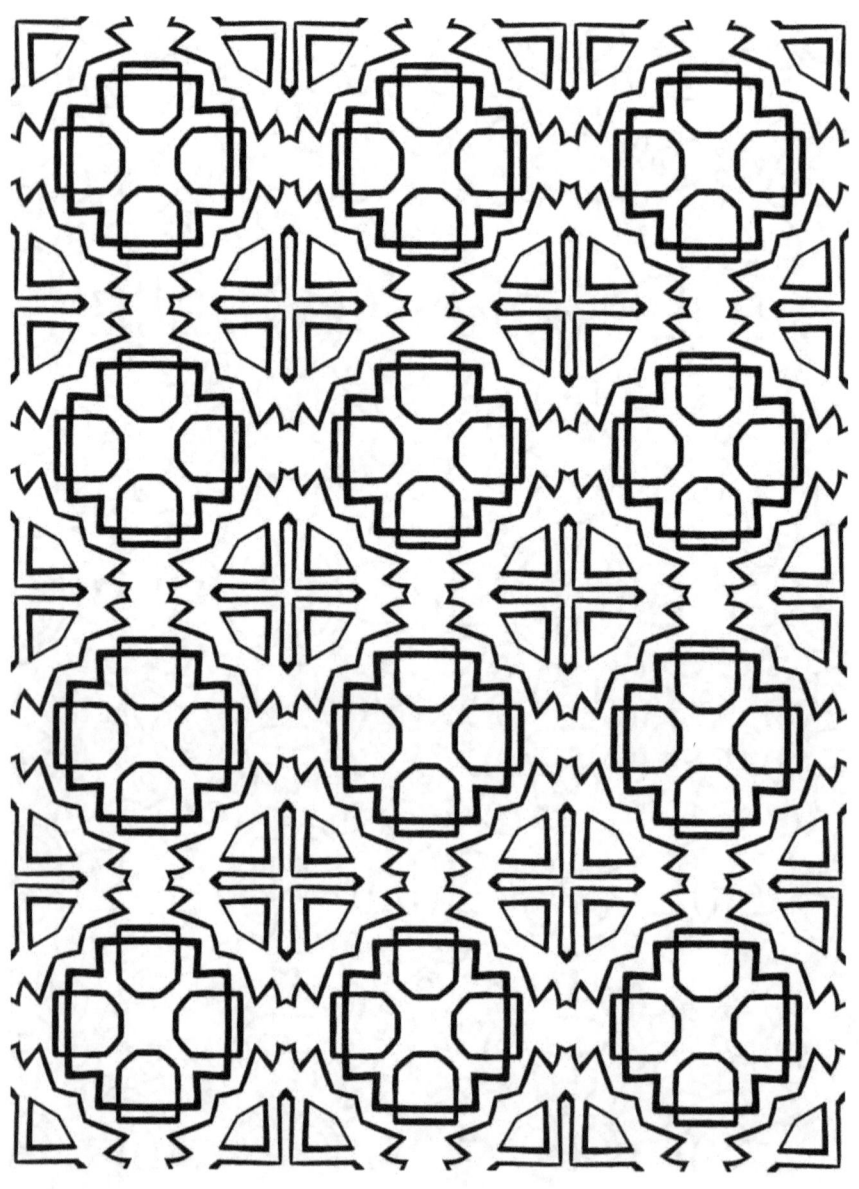

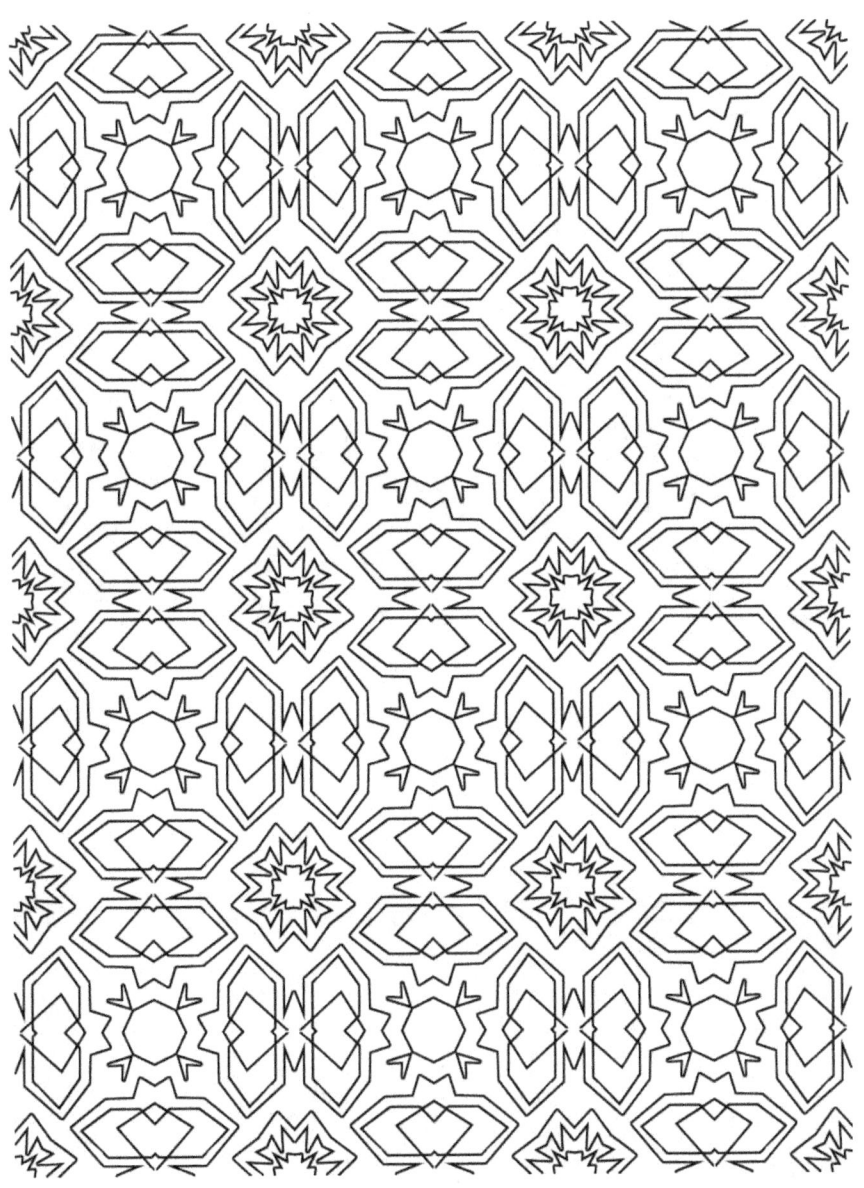

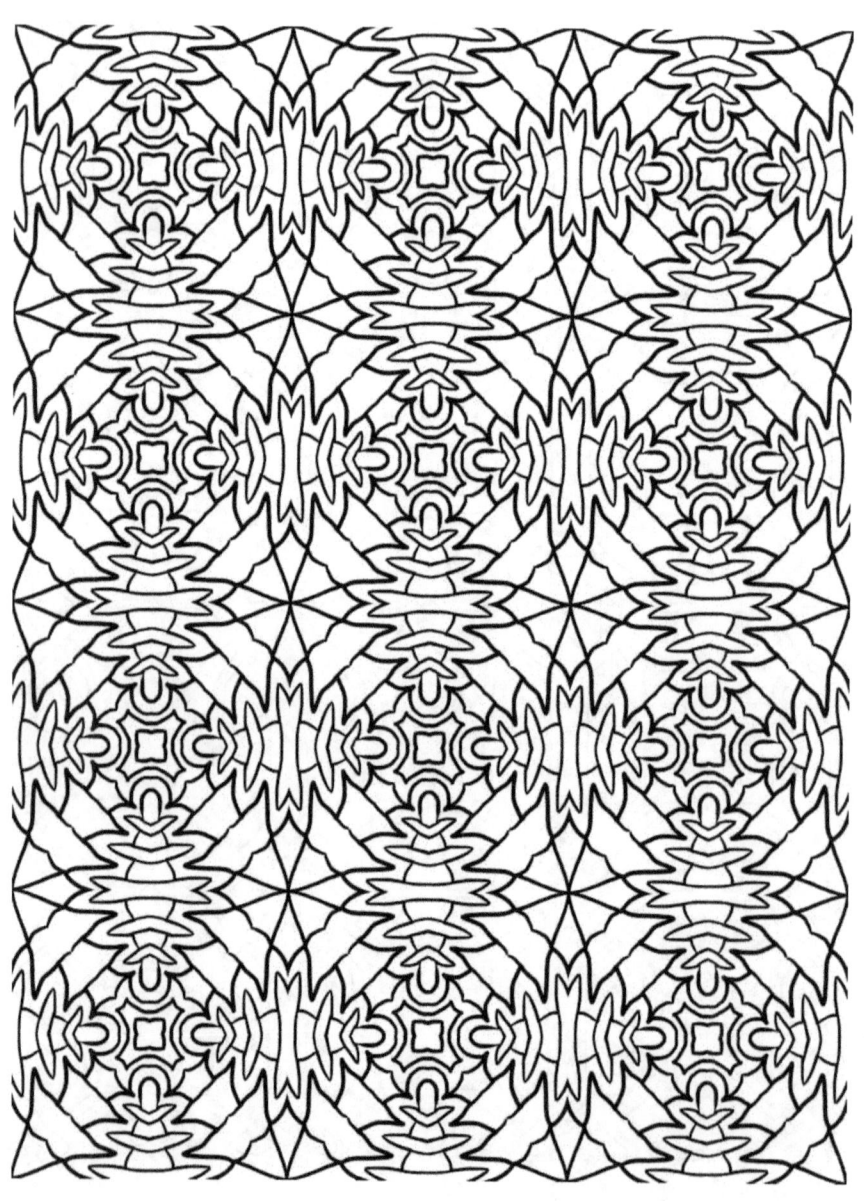

You Can Check Out My Other Coloring Books & Other Books By Searching My Name (Dorothy Mohl) On Amazon. If You Liked The Book, I Would Appreciate If You Posted A Review On Amazon.

Thank You! I hope You Enjoyed!

www.ingramcontent.com/pod-product-compliance
Lightning Source LLC
Chambersburg PA
CBHW070224210526
45169CB00024B/1535